The Path to Harness Racing Handicapping Profits

One Man's Journey to Success

Douglas Masters

Disclaimer

Although the author and publisher have made every effort to ensure that the information in this book was correct at press time, the author and publisher do not assume and hereby disclaim any liability to any party for any loss, damage, or disruption caused by errors or omissions, whether such errors or omissions result from negligence, accident, or any other cause.

Table of Contents

Other publications from Teela Books

Introduction

I have been handicapping and betting on harness racing for 30 years, but this wasn't always the case. I had been a fan of thoroughbred racing for some time but showed no interest in harness racing. Living in Southern California meant that I was experiencing top quality thoroughbred racing. Harness racing, on the other hand, seemed to be a sport that was losing interest with the public. Harness racing at Hollywood Park had come to an end. But in the early 1980s, there was resurgence in harness racing. More racing dates had been assigned to Los Alamitos, and since I lived close by, I decided to take a first-hand look at harness racing.

I was immediately captivated by the sport. I noticed from the beginning that it was quite different from thoroughbred racing. With rare exception, all of the races were carded at the same one mile distance, and there was a much greater pace to the races. Standardbreds would often finish faster than they started. Although thoroughbreds would have closers in a race, the horses that finished well were usually not finishing the race faster but passing tiring horses. The strong finish in thoroughbred racing was an illusion. With standardbreds, a horse could go the first three quarters of a mile in 30 seconds per quarter but finish the last quarter in 28 seconds. I found this to be fascinating. Standardbreds were truly pacing, and I thought these times might lend themselves well to pace handicapping much more so than with thoroughbreds. After watching three or four races, another aspect of harness racing that jumped out was how much the trip affected the outcome of the race. Although the occasional bad trip could hurt a thoroughbred's chance of winning, it was much more pronounced in a harness race. It became clear that a past performance line for a harness horse that looked terrible was much different when seen in person. Horses that went wide with a sulky were moving farther to the outside than a thoroughbred would. I quickly understood that post positions were more influential on the outcome of a race than in thoroughbred racing and often contributed to the type of trip a horse experienced.

The importance of the trip and post position led to an appreciation of the driver and the influence drivers had on the outcome of the race. Drivers with more ability gave horses a better chance of winning as they showed the ability to give a horse a better trip during the race.

These were only a few of my observations, and this after only one night at the track. I started coming back again and again. At first I would note the race in my program for each quarter and noted which horses seemed to be in the best shape whether they won the race or not. When these horses came back next week to race, I was able to look at the notes I had in my program to determine which horses had the best chance in tonight's race. I was able to pick winners directly from my program notes without looking at the past performance lines.

After this, I started bringing my binoculars to the track to pay attention to the horses warming up earlier in the program and right before the race. I slowly stopped doing this as it didn't produce many winners and may have interfered with my observational handicapping with program notes. After this, I became somewhat obsessed with statistics and began to get a grasp of which factors in a particle type of race were most important. These statistics, combined with a pace rating method I developed, helped to augment my observation handicapping. To this day, if I were to bet only one track, this would be my preferred method. However, it can be time consuming and is not compatible with betting several race tracks each evening, and that is what happened in the 1990s.

Harness racing was beamed in from other states, and there were an entirely new group of drivers and conditions creating whole new outcomes for the races. Trips to Las Vegas brought even more harness tracks, and I began to work toward a different method of handicapping that allowed for a large number of races to be bet across many racetracks.

By the late 1990s, I was showing a profit betting all satellite signals except one. I continued to show a profit, locally. With my trips to Las Vegas I showed a profit on my betting as a whole but did not necessarily show a profit on every track I was betting.

By the turn of the century, I was living in Las Vegas and was fine tuning my handicapping to the point where I had a healthy return on my bets. Just as casinos have an advantage in the games they offer, I too had an advantage over harness racing, and my handicapping became only a question of making the right bets and enough bets.

After 30 years of handicapping, I have built up a reservoir of knowledge on my approach to the game. Some of what I have learned on my path to success may be helpful to you, but then again it may not. It depends upon your current level of success and your method of handicapping. There is more than one way to make a profit betting harness racing, and your way may be different from mine. However, for those who are beginners or intermediate handicappers, you may learn a few things that will improve your game.

One word of warning for those who are beginners, I have not taken the time to explain the basics of harness racing. This includes terminology. Most harness programs have a glossary and other basic knowledge you can learn from. There is also good information for beginners at the website of the United States Trotting Association.

I have begun with the factors I consider important in harness racing. Some I have given more importance to than others, but there are some that are more important from a betting perspective than a statistical one. Many handicapping factors are well known to the general harness betting public and are already baked into the odds. Using this type of handicapping knowledge doesn't help much if it isn't going to result in making money in the long run.

No winning examples in this book

You will find no past performances listed in this book; this is intentional. Anyone who has been around harness racing for even a few years has probably read various books and publications offering a handicapping system. All of them will have examples of how a handicapping system or angle picked a winner. Anyone can do this, especially when so many of these authors are working backwards from the winner. To me, it is simply a waste of time. And besides, only a mediocre or inexperienced handicapper is going to believe there is a single path to success in wagering. This book consists of my observations of the sport and how it relates to my own handicapping perspective. If you are looking for a system that represents some sort of absolute truth, you're looking in the wrong place.

Handicapping and betting on harness races is no different from any other competitive endeavor. Successful people have different styles and different levels of ability. This is true in sports such as baseball, basketball and football, but it is equally true with lawyers, accountants and doctors. At best, you can only seek to improve your skills and therefore, improve your game.

Section 1

Handicapping Factors

Drivers

This is a big factor in determining which horse will win the race or at least the probability of the horse wining. Unfortunately, every one knows this, and the top drivers will usually go off at low odds when they have a good horse. A poor driver could drive around one turn and find ways to lose the race. Winning drivers simply have more ability than those with lower ratings and win percentages.

There was a time when I only bet one or two tracks, I would rate the drivers on a letter grade scale. The very best were given an A grade, the good drivers a B and the mediocre drivers a C. Poor drivers were all labeled a D. What I found over time, both from my records and observation, was that A rated drivers would typically improve the horse's chance of winning. It wasn't so much they made the horse pace faster, but that they were able to drive in a way that gave a horse a better chance of winning. Common examples would be preventing a horse from being boxed in entering the stretch or being able to flush cover when parked out. Unfortunately, the grade A drivers were usually bet heavily. It was the B and C drivers that produced the overlays in my betting. However, with enough observation and note taking, I was able to realize that drivers had strengths and weaknesses. Some drivers were able to drive cheaper horses best while other drivers were better with higher class pacers. Some drivers had a knack for success with fillies and mares while others were great with closers. After a while I understood how important the skills of the driver were. The crowd would bet down the lone speed horse in a race without realizing that the particular driver in the sulky was terrible with a horse on the lead.

The following examples only scratch the surface of the skills of top drivers as well as the skills lacking with mediocre and poor drivers.

*When leaving at the start, knowing when to challenge for the lead or tuck-in along the rail

*Being able to give a horse a breather when pacing on the lead

*When a driver's horse is in the lead, knowing whether to keep a challenger parked out or let him take the lead then re-take later.

*If pacing second on the rail, knowing how good the leading horse is and when to make a move.

*Knowing how to flush live cover when moving first over early in the race.

*Knowing if and when to go three wide with a live horse.

*Being able to judge how live the cover is of a first over horse

when pacing second over. Unless a horse is strong, a driver may have to go three wide before he wants to.

*Challenging a slow pace in the 2nd quarter. The lead horse may be weak, and the driver is trying to steal the race with a slow pace.

*Judging how fast or slow the early pace is. If it is too quick for a particular class level, a driver needs to know when to make his move.

*Knowing the other driver's tendencies. Often the drivers are playing a poker game during the race. They may not know the other driver's horse in a particular race, but they are familiar with how the driver plays the game.

Conclusion

It is important to know your drivers. The best course of action is to handicap the horse's chances first, and then look at the driver. Often good drivers will be underbet while the popular drivers are bet down and produce underlays that should be avoided.

Condition or Shape

A horse can only maintain peak condition for a certain period of time. It may be one or two races, as is the case with low priced claimers, or it can be several races that are commonly seen with higher class horses. Once a horse begins to tail off, it will need some time off or at least an easy race or two. When a horse is not in peak form, the horse is referred to as being short, and it will not be expected by the trainer to pace its best race tonight. The horse may be short for many reasons, but from a betting point of view, it is only necessary to eliminate the short horses and identify the horses in good shape for tonight's race.

To identify a horse in good shape, most of the time the last performance line will be enough; however, if a horse paced poorly in its last race, I will go to the second race back. Provided that this second race back was in the last three weeks. I might go four weeks if the horse's last race was two weeks ago, but this is as far as I will take it. The reason I do this is because a horse may have had a good excuse for a poor performance in its last race. There are different reasons for this, and many of the reasons are not apparent in the program, but only to those who saw the last race. There are also situations where only the trainer may know the reason for the poor race, and in some circumstances, no one will know. Often a horse throws in a bad race for an unknown reason, and this reason will not affect the horse's performance tonight. Horses that have a good race two back in their performance lines, but have a poor last race, are the source of many good overlays.

Cheap horses have a difficult time maintaining anything that resembles a form cycle. Low priced horses are not only slower than higher priced horses, but they often have a lot more physical problems. They may pace a good race but have a difficult time putting together two good races back to back. For this reason, cheap horses are difficult to handicap and represent a specialty for many harness handicappers.

Often a horse will achieve a lifetime mark for a win in its last race. This represents a peak condition that will most likely drop off in the horse's next start. Three year old horses are often an exception as they are still growing. Older horses will seldom be able to hold their form off a peak lifetime effort. The older the horse is, the bigger the drop in form in its next race. For older horses, I usually eliminate a horse whose last race was its fastest. There are three ways to determine this. You can look at the comment line if there is one, but the second way is to look at the final time of the horse's win and compare that to the lifetime mark listed in the top right position of the past performances.

Determining current condition

Determining a horse's current condition or shape can be tricky and takes time to master. But it is an art, and the best you can achieve is to be right about a horse's condition most of the time. There are basic things to look for in the past performances. The first is a recent race. Standardbreds can pace once a week when healthy, but there are a variety of reasons why a horse may skip a week. Sometimes a trainer just wants to give a horse a break from racing, but the horse is still working out and staying in shape. Perhaps a race was not available for the horse or maybe the weather or track was not good for the horse. There can be many reasons for missing a week of racing, and I will always give a horse the benefit of the doubt. However, after two weeks, there may have been a problem with the horse, and even if there was no problem, the horse may not be in peak form for tonight's race. I will not bet on a horse that has not paced in the last two weeks.

A horse needs to have shown some work in its last race. This means the horse needs to have been leading at some point in the race or challenged first over for the lead during the race. If the horse was pacing second or third over, it should have shown some progress in the stretch run. The same is true with a horse that paced along the rail; it should show progress in the stretch. This means a gain in position, lengths behind or both. When a horse has not shown any work during a race, it is most likely out of shape. It is possible that the horse was pacing at a class level that is too high for it to be competitive, but a horse will usually show some signs of life at a higher class level than it will be pacing at tonight.

Speed

Differences in temperatures from night and day racing can influence final time greatly. Differences in temperatures from one night to the next can also have an influence on final times. Because of changing weather, the track may vary in how fast or slow it is. If a handicapper is inclined to use speed ratings, good track variants must be used as well as a good knowledge of expected final times for each class of horse that is pacing in each race to construct track variants.

Although many use speed ratings, I don't like them much. They ignore class and the way a race is paced. A fast or slow final time can be deceiving as the final time has a lot to do with the early fractions of the race. It also fails to consider troubled trips a horse may have in a race. The final time may be deceptively slow if the favorite was interfered with by a breaking horse and finished poorly. This same horse may have won the race by a full second faster without the interference.

Speed ratings, like other types of ratings such as pace, class or consistency, have usefulness to a handicapper, but you need to understand their limitations. I seldom use ratings for horses, and when I do, I use them after I have eliminated horses I consider to be those that will produce a negative return on my wagers. This is helpful, because I am often throwing out a horse that looks good on its rating but represents a bad bet.

Pace

I consider pace ratings to be superior to speed ratings, but they still only show you a performance measured on a certain day. They do not predict what will happen in tonight's race, but they can be very helpful. Like speed ratings, you need to use track variants for pace ratings. I often use pace ratings in my handicapping for the purpose of determining a horse's condition as well as to help project how the race will be run.

Pace ratings, when constructed properly, will show how fast a horse can pace early and produce a certain final time. When two horses can produce equal final times, it is the horse that can pace a faster early speed fraction that has more ability.

Pace ratings can be especially useful to determine how much pressure there will be on the front end of the race. If there is too much early speed, this will benefit horses that are closers. This is obvious enough to most handicappers, but often there will be three or four horses with early speed in a race, and it may look like there is a speed duel that will develop. But when analyzed with pace figures, it becomes clear that one horse is the speed of the speed. The other early speed horses are simply overmatched on pace. Good overlays can be found with pace ratings in this type of situation.

Notes on race classification and class

Although there are many handicapping factors, the classification of the race is where the entire handicapping process begins. This is true because you need to know what approach to take in analyzing a race. No one method of handicapping is so all encompassing that it applies to every race on the program. Different class levels will place an emphasis on different handicapping factors.

The Path to Harness Racing Handicapping Profits

There are many levels of harness racing and certain races need a stronger emphasis on one handicapping factor over another. In some cases, such as the lowest class levels, it can be difficult to find a bet at all. Every race track will have their lowest class level, and it is here that you will find horses that have little hope of winning. Their only chance to win is to be shipped to a lower class racetrack with even cheaper horses.

After reaching peak form, lower price claiming horses may only maintain it for as little as one week. All horses at these lower levels will have a variety of problems, and some of them will get worse seemingly overnight. Often, this can happen after one good race. For this reason, it is difficult to find good bets at these lower levels.

A horse jumping in class from its last race may not be going up in class. This is commonly seen when a horse paces to a win in its last race but was dropping into the race from its previous race. A horse winning off a class drop can often move up easily because its penultimate race and races further back were at tonight's level or better.

A horse dropping from a higher class race in its last few races to today's race may not be dropping in class. A horse that has shown little effort in higher class races may not be competitive in today's lower class race. The trainer may still be looking for the horse's proper level.

A horse can race too high for too long and become jaded. It is as if the horse has had its mind blown, and when dropped to what should be its competitive level, the horse shows nothing. This is a mistake on the part of the trainer. Knowing your horse is a part of success.

A horse showing a good final time at a higher class has usually been sucked along. It has paced with the herd as best it can, but given a chance to go to the lead or challenge first over, this same horse's final time will drop significantly Horses often will slow down if they have to pace competitively. However, many horses can wake up and pace a mile that is better than they have paced in a long time. Sometimes they will win tonight's race posting a lifetime mark. When this happens, a horse will usually show some signs of life against better competition in its last race or two. The exception is when a horse is dropping more than one level. When a horse wakes up to pace a monster race with a class drop, it is usually a double drop or better, and this drop is from its last several races not just the last race.

The Path to Harness Racing Handicapping Profits

Racing grinds away on a horse. Every horse is different, but on average, they seem to reach their peak at age five. From this point in time it is downhill. A race horse will go up and down over time in class level, but the trend is downward. Occasionally you will see a horse catch fire and win race after race as it goes up in class each week, but if you go back in time and look at the animal's lifetime, past performance lines, inevitably you will find that the horse paced in much higher class races. The recent turnaround may have been due to a problem the horse had for a long time, but was finally corrected, giving the horse a second wind in its racing career. Although bettors don't see this in the last few races listed in a program, most likely the horse will have back class.

It is important to be able to judge a horse's class, and there are many ways to construct class ratings to measure this. Class ratings that use the purse as a determination of class can be deceptive. A horse pacing for $20,000 purse money at Pocono Downs then moving to the Meadowlands for a purse of $14,000 is not necessarily dropping in class and may find the competition too tough. Although the purse value of the race indicates class in general, it does not apply to a specific race. A claiming race restricted to state bred horses may have a higher purse than one that is open to all horses, but this latter race will most likely be tougher than a state bred race. I have played around with different methods to determine a class rating over the years, but in the end, I ended up with an elimination method that allows me to wager on horses that are competitive at tonight's level. I have outlined this concept later in the book when I discuss my method of handicapping.

Post position

Post positions can be a valuable handicapping factor but not in the normal way people view them. Every track program has the post position numbers listed in their program, so everyone is aware of the posts that are good and bad. Of course, the way the data is listed in a program does not indicate the extent the post is good or bad. The numbers listed are usually for starts and wins with a win percentage calculated. To get a better idea as to how well each post is, you need to calculate the expectation of the number of wins for each post and compare this with the number of wins. The outside posts have fewer races and will therefore produce fewer wins. The bottom line is that some post positions are worse than people realize and others better. However, it is generally true that the outside post positions are the worst in any full field at a harness track. Like many handicapping factors, bettors are aware of this; however, overlays due to post position can often be found in the outside posts because bettors have a tendency to believe the outside post positions are worse than they actually are.

There are times when post position statistics can be thrown out. If there are two early speed horses, regardless of the specific statistics for a track, the driver on the inside will have the advantage. Assuming, of course, the driver has the skills to recognize and take advantage of this situation.

Many times a horse with a bad post position will not be sent. The trainer decides that he doesn't want to rough up the horse with a tough race and thinks it is better to wait until next week to go for the win. It is not like the trainer is instructing the driver to throw the race; it is just that the horse will be taken back from the outside, and the driver will try to find an easy spot on the rail. The driver will usually move at the half but will be too far behind to win especially if the pace was slow. A good finish will keep the horse in shape for next week's race, and maybe the horse will get a better post position. You may have seen this many times before; it usually happens when a horse gets stuck outside for two or more races. Although most bettors will notice the post switch, it will be under bet as a factor in the outcome of the race. This is because the previous race or two were not as competitive as a bettor wants to see.

The public wants to see early speed from the outside in the horse's last race, then a move to an inside post in tonight's race. Often, a horse will have a closing effort in its last race, and this helps to keep the odds higher after the post switch. Of course, what happens is the horse shows good early speed in tonight's race from the inside post.

The main lesson from my years of handicapping harness racing is to be aware of the probabilities for post position at the track I'm handicapping but not use it as a crutch in handicapping the races. Good payoffs are waiting for the smart bettor on horses leaving from the outside post positions.

Track

Know your track but know other tracks as well. Often harness bettors get too wrapped up in their own home track and fail to appreciate that harness racing exists outside of their track. Horses from another track may seem to have a class edge and are bet down to low odds, but do poorly because the class doesn't translate to the local track. Other horses may seem to be going up in class, but turn out to be very competitive. Knowing how horses fare when shipping from one track to another is an important aspect of handicapping. Some horses can be eliminated based upon their recent races at another track while some become automatic contenders. Knowing which horse is which can help eliminate horses from contention and find overlays in the betting.

Equally important is to know how a horse will pace when shipping in from a particular track. Speed and pace ratings can be deceptive in this type of situation. A shipper may have superior pace or speed figures, but from experience, you know that horses arriving from a particular track do not perform well. Or horses shipping from a particular track tend to be competitive, but only after a race or two over the local oval. Other tracks may produce live horses with a good chance at winning in their first race. More commonly, how well a horse does will depend on the class level it competed in at its previous track and how that compares to the race it is competing in tonight. A horse may do well shipping in from a particular track if it is a mid-level claiming animal, but anything higher in class is an automatic elimination. The only way to get a handle on what is happening at any particular track is to keep accurate records of shippers and how well they fared. There is no substitute for this type of approach.

Knowing the contour of the racetrack and the dimensions are

important as well. A horse shipping in from another track may have a better chance of winning simply because today's track favors the horse's pacing style. The horse may be an early speed type that has been fading on a mile track, but now is competing at a five-eighths oval; this smaller oval may help his early speed last longer, maybe even to the finish line.

Age and Sex

I have done statistics years ago on age for several racetracks, and the results have always been inconclusive. Although in claiming races and condition races, the older horses have a slight advantage; it is just the opposite with non-winners type races. Races carded for non-winners of 1, 2, 3 or more favor the three year old but only slightly. Three year old horses can improve dramatically as they are still growing; however, they show less improvement when competing in claiming type races. At best, both age and sex are minor factors, and I usually ignore them. However, I do favor the younger three year olds in non-winners races that are not eligible to be claimed. You do have to be careful with this. Trainers and owners are often looking to simply keep a horse in good shape between stakes races. They will not attempt to go all out to win a race that will hurt the horse's shape, making it more difficult to win a part of a much larger purse next week. An example of this would be having an outside post position and not fighting for the lead. The horse is taken back early and then paces a strong final half or quarter. Or a horse has an inside post position, but stays on the rail until the stretch run. The horse loses but will be in good shape to compete for a stakes purse against its own age next week. In short, be careful betting three year old stakes horses when pacing for smaller purses.

On the upper end of the scale, I will seldom bet a horse over 10 years of age. At some tracks there are a plethora of horses in the double digits, so you may want to analyze the ages for a specific track. I have found that I don't lose enough bets to warrant any special research. Regardless of which track I am betting, I seldom get beat by horses 12 and older. I should be quick to point out that I do not eliminate for age, but if my top bet is too old, I may pass the race.

Trainer

I do not put a lot of emphasis on the trainer in my handicapping as a stand alone factor. In other words, I will not eliminate a horse from contention because of the trainer. However, when I am looking at the horse's present shape and class, I try to put myself in the shoes of a trainer to get an idea of why the horse is in tonight's race and what a trainer hopes to accomplish in tonight's race. This doesn't always help because many trainers don't seem to know what they are doing.

The one time I take a long look at a trainer is when there are trainer changes due to claims. Unlike many handicappers, I am not looking to determine how much improvement the new trainer can get from a horse relative to the previous trainer, but I am looking at the potential for a horse to drop in performance. A trainer change from one with a lot of talent to one that is poor or mediocre can make a horse's past performance look much better than it will demonstrate for the new barn. If my leading contender has a negative trainer change, I may pass the race, but depending upon how bad the trainer is, I may simply throw the horse out from contention.

In general, I discount a horse's performance if there has been a change from a good trainer to a mediocre or poor one. I have seen horses' performances drop off significantly with a simple barn change.

Section 2

Statistics

Handicappers, including myself, can get to the point where they believe something is true in the world of harness handicapping but may not be true at all. There is no better way to learn something than to gather your own data and analyze it. I have always shunned data that is provided to me. I do not trust it. Too often people have an ax to grind and are only trying to prove a point they already believe is true. The one exception is post position data that is provided in a race track's program, but even in this case, it is the raw data I am using and not the analysis in the program. I can analyze the data better myself.

Never change your handicapping method based upon a couple of losing bets. Perhaps you had a raced narrowed to only two contenders, and you bet the losing horse. You say to yourself that it was because you bet the three year old versus an older horse, or perhaps you bet a shipper and now believe all horses from this other racetrack should be avoided. Don't start changing your method without any evidence to justify the change. Although you may want to suspend wagering in these uncertain situations until you can get good information. Start gathering your own numbers and decide for yourself what the truth is. You can gather data for all tracks or just the ones you are betting. Keep your programs and start recording the results. If you want data faster, you can use race charts or old programs. I have recorded a lot of data over the years just to learn something, so I was not dependent on my intuition and a few races of observation. Recording your own data and analyzing it can be a rewarding experience and will help your handicapping.

The Path to Harness Racing Handicapping Profits

I only took a semester of statistics in college, so the statistical work I have done in the past was limited. I simply recorded the results of a particular parameter of harness racing and compared that with the random expectation. For example, looking at age in maiden races, I would record the number of horses that competed by age in a couple of hundred races as well as the age of the winning horse. I could then calculate the percentage of each age as it was represented in the data and the percentage of winners by age. Each age should win about the same percentage as it was represented. Often the numbers would be quite different depending upon the specific attribute I was analyzing. To determine how significant this difference was, I would use a statistical test. For most harness data, the t-test was the most appropriate.

I have discovered interesting things about harness racing over the years, but be forewarned, most of the valuable information has been track specific. There have been good numbers I have generated that apply to harness racing in general, but these factors are things that good players pick up over time just by watching and handicapping the races. If you have never attempted your own statistical analysis before, start with a particular track. You can always expand your analysis by gathering data on other tracks to see if a new gem of information applies to other racetracks.

Section 3

Wagering

Although many do not think of wagering as a handicapping factor, it is not only a factor, but one of the most important of the entire process. You can be the greatest handicapper ever, but if you do not know how to wager, you will be a losing player. Assuming you are a handicapper that can pick strong contenders in a harness race at overlay odds, there is still the question of how to bet the race. Your wagering should reflect both your handicapping method and your temperament. Some handicappers, like me, prefer the straight pool. In particular, I always bet to win and place on a single horse. Others may want to bet only to win and still others prefer the exotic pools such as the exacta or trifecta.

My preference for splitting my wager between win and place is based upon the fact that I have a strong return on investment betting this way. Part of it is psychological, but I recognize this and adapt to my temperament for wagering money. When I examine my bets, I always show greater profits on the win bet. It would be easy to conclude that I should only bet to win and maximize my profits. Unfortunately, in the real world, it doesn't work that way. Once I begin to bet only to win, my returns drop significantly lower. This may have to do with the losing streaks being longer in the win column, and this shakes my confidence in my handicapping. By betting to place, it is easier to withstand the losing streaks. Whatever the reason is, it is mostly psychological. The important thing to understand is that I adapt to whatever weakness I have as a handicapper. It is much better to be a winning bettor with win and place wagers than to eke out smaller profits, break even or lose money betting to win only.

I have shown some success at betting doubles and pick 4s, but with these bets, I am still picking winners. With wagers like exactas I am trying to pick a second place finisher and with trifectas I am attempting to pick the first three finishers. My handicapping doesn't see harness racing in this manner, and I don't attempt to win with these types of bets. Naturally, I have made these types of bets in the past. In fact, over the years I have won many exactas and a few trifectas that I had to sign for, but I have never shown much profit.

28

Section 4

Keeping records

This is absolutely essential to winning in the long run. Keeping accurate records of my wagers has been the key factor in transforming from a losing bettor to a break even bettor, and from break even, I produced single digit advantage numbers over the game, then moved into the double digits that I have enjoyed for several years. The type of records I keep are for each bet I make, how much and the type of bet it is. I record the track, date of race, race number and the type of race I bet. In the past, I also included the horse's name as well as the post position the horse started from, and of course, the driver was entered. Naturally, the result of the horse's performance, as well as the bet, was recorded.

If you do this as I did, after a hundred bets or so, patterns will begin to emerge. You may discover that you are a better handicapper than you think. If you stop betting certain types of races, suddenly your losses diminish. If there are areas of handicapping you a struggling with, then simply suspend your wagering in these situations until you can improve that aspect of your game. One of my early discoveries was there were two drivers I wagered entirely too often. These were drivers that were losing their races and taking my money with their loss.

Knowing what your strengths and weaknesses are as a handicapper will help you play to your strengths as well as point to the areas where you can work to improve your game, but there is a second aspect to record keeping that is essential for success. This is in knowing whether you are winning or losing player and what your advantage or disadvantage is with harness betting as well as to what extent it is.

Without good record keeping, it becomes too easy to fool yourself into thinking you are doing better than you are. Here in my home town of Las Vegas locals gamble a lot of money. There is so much money gambled that there are many nice casinos that are dedicated to the local customer. However, if most of these people were asked how they did with their gambling, they will most likely say they are a little ahead or have broken even. Usually, this is an honest answer. Regardless of what game is being played, few people keep track of their wins and losses. Harness bettors are no different, and they often think they are doing much better than they are.

Of course, with most casino games, you are playing against the house and cannot win in the long run. Harness racing is pari-mutuel and is a game that can be beaten. You are playing against other bettors and need to have more skill than they do to overcome a 16 to 19 percent track take and become a winning player. It can be done, but you need accurate records to know what your level of play is and have the data to help point you in the winning direction. If you are a baseball player and want to improve your hitting, you need to know what your batting average is right now, so you will have a point of reference and can measure whether you are improving. Again, because harness betting is pari-mutuel, you can improve your skills relative to other players and become a winning player. The secret is in betting horses that are overlays.

Regardless of your method of handicapping, you can never know with any certainty that any one wager was a good bet. You may think a horse going off at 4-1 is a great overlay and should be going off at 2-1. When the horse wins, you will pat yourself on the back, but how do you know that it was an overlay? The truth is that you can never know what the exact probability is of any horse winning any race. You can only look at the aggregate information. You will not know the specific probability of a horse winning, but your records will show that when you bet a horse in a particular situation with your handicapping method, you will show a certain percentage profit over the course of many wagers. It is entirely possible that some of the bets were not overlays and others were much greater than your average return, but what is important is that when looking at certain parameters of a race, you are able to show a profit.

Once you have recorded a hundred or more bets, you will begin to see patterns emerge. Certain types of racing will be obvious losing propositions for you. At this point, you must avoid deceiving yourself into thinking that you could have done much better if you would not have made a few mistakes. Your focus should not be on areas that you did poorly, but on those races you did well. Maybe it is a type of race or a particular race track you do well at, this is where you must focus your attention. The area where you showed a profit or at least the area you had the smallest losing percentage should be the focal point of your handicapping. Try to improve your game in the areas that are most productive for you. In time, as you get better, you can expand to other types of races. But always keep in mind, you will probably never master every aspect of harness race betting, and it is better to accept this now, so you can put yourself in the black as soon as possible.

Section 5

Betting multiple racetracks

Here in Las Vegas, we do not have racetracks and cannot bet across state lines; we are limited to whatever the race books offer. However, this still represents a smorgasbord of harness tracks to bet on. Now, in the age of satellite wagering, many harness players have this same opportunity outside of Nevada. With the growth of off-track wagering, there are several tracks to choose from betting at your local track as well as satellite facilities. There is also online betting available in many states as well. The advantage of having several tracks to wager on is obvious to the handicapper with an advantage over the game. In the past, it has always been frustrating to only have a couple of races that offer profit potential, but now, even a program with two or three good bets can be multiplied by six or seven tracks. An advantage over the game quickly begins to generate serious returns to a horse player's bankroll.

Know your drivers. Each track will have their top drivers, and anyone who is consistently betting a particular track will know who they are regardless of how high in the standings they appear. However, many of the harness tracks in the east are close together, and a top driver from one track will show up at another track. If the driver is in the top three at the other track, he may get noticed in the betting, but just as often, he will not. The real overlays in visiting drivers are ones that have good win percentages at their home track but have a lower win percentage at the visiting track. The lower win percentage driver may be a reflection of a lower number of starts and does not reflect the driver's ability.

When I am betting several racetracks at a time, I am looking to establish a positive return on my bets then grind out profits by betting as many races as possible. Of course, at all times I have to keep in mind not to force the bet. Making all possible eliminations leaves me in a position of having a positive return on races that I wager on. An analysis of which horses have the best chance of winning tonight's race along with their odds increases the advantage over the game.

How many races do I bet on a typical card? It depends upon the track and the particular night of racing. Some tracks card two year old and trotting races in greater numbers on certain nights. Typically, I am making wagers on two to five races per track. Depending upon how many tracks I am betting, this can add up to a significant number of wagers. This is why I handicap well before I arrive at the race book. The past performances I use, downloaded from the Internet, are superior to the ones in the program, so I benefit from this over most of the bettors using the track programs. Once I get to the race book, I only need to make note of changes in the program. I wait for the wagering to begin on a race I am interested in and follow the odds. Depending upon weather conditions, scratches, driver changes and closing odds, I will probably pass a few races I planned on betting.

If you are serious about betting several race tracks, I would recommend using the past performances that are purchased online and can be viewed in pdf format. Trackmaster is a company that provides harness past performances, and they have track variants available in each horse's past performance line. The variants are usually good numbers to work with. I get no compensation for endorsing their product, but this is certainly a good place to start for obtaining past performance data. You may be able to find better track variants elsewhere.

Section 6

Winter Racing

It is easy to simply advise people not to bet harness racing in the winter time, but there are two problems with that. The first is that winter racing continues to grow, and with more tracks offering more races, a growing number of people are betting on harness racing in the winter. The second problem is that it is too tempting for me; I bet on harness racing in the winter. To advise against it would be hypocritical. You need to keep in mind that it is more difficult to make a profit in the winter. The horses are cheaper, and the racing can be unpredictable. But you can be successful if you keep a couple of things in mind.

Never bet when it is raining or snowing. A few snow flurries that don't affect the visibility for the driver is okay, but once it begins coming down hard, pass the race. The same is true with rain. When it is cold in the winter, rain can turn to sleet. Granted, the racetrack will suspend racing until it passes, but you do not want this to happen, even on a small scale, during the race.

A track doesn't have to be labeled fast, but you want at least a good track. Harness tracks hold up well to weather and have a better consistency than seen with other breeds of horse racing. Above all, be patient. Patience is a virtue under optimal race conditions, but in the winter time, it takes on additional significance.

Section 7

Things that trip up a beginner

or

Weaknesses I have had in the past

as a harness handicapper

Because I kept notes from my earliest days of handicapping, I can go back in time and see some of the mistakes that I made. Avoiding these mistakes would have saved me a great deal of money, and they may be of value to you as well.

Betting too many races

Betting races that my handicapping methods produced no contenders or too many contenders cost me money. By keeping records, or at least your old programs, you will be able to see the bad bets materialize before your eyes. But even without records, any time you are not sure that you are making a good wager, walk away from the race. Not losing money unnecessarily helps your bottom line.

Passing a race, then thinking you had the winner

I was guilty of this, and it can become a real problem. After handicapping a race, I may have two to four contenders, and even though I lean towards one of the horses, I pass on betting the race. Naturally the horse I was leaning towards wins the race. I would then think that I had the winner and should have made the bet, but the truth is, once I have decided not to bet the race, I didn't have the winner or loser. I had to discipline myself to think that way. Once the decision to pass a race has been made, it is over. There is no second guessing. The race can be watched, but there is nothing being bet and there can be no "what if" scenario on my part. It reminds me of poker. When a player folds his hand and his opponent wins, he will often want to see what the other player had. But it doesn't matter what the other player had, it was the winning hand. That is all that matters. If you pass a race, it doesn't matter which horse won; you did not have a financial interest in the race; therefore, you did not have the winner.

If the horse I handicapped on top of the race scratched from the race, I would often bet my next choice, but this was a mistake. It is better to walk away from the race. My records indicated early in my betting career that I did not make a profit on races when I had to bet my second choice after my first choice scratched. Of course, many years later, I don't have choices that are ranked from best to least, but I think in terms of odds and probabilities.

Too much emphasis on post position

Without doubt, post position can have a large impact on the outcome of a race. But there are two problems with using it as a handicapping factor. The first is that it can easily be overemphasized as to the influence it will have on the outcome of a race. Often horses with poor post positions can do well in a race and those with good positions can end up pacing a troubled race. It is simply a matter of probability, and as such, this factor is one that falls somewhere between a major and a minor handicapping factor. Most important of all is the fact that even a person with average handicapping skills can calculate the effect of the post position on a race, so the odds already reflect this factor. Seldom can a good handicapper find overlays with post position being the major factor. Post position should only be a factor in projecting how the race will be paced.

Driver changes

This is a factor that can fool both the beginner and seasoned harness player. A top driver can move a horse up two or three lengths when taking over from a poor or mediocre driver. However, you must be careful with driver changes and not get caught up in the changes to the point where they become a major handicapping factor. A top driver may have a choice between two horses and leave one in favor of the other. Your handicapping may put the horse he is not driving tonight as the one with the better chance. However, you jump on the bandwagon and follow the driver instead of the horse. The reason a driver chooses one horse over another may not have anything to do with which horse the driver thinks will win. Often it is due to the trainer. A top driver may drive for a certain trainer as he is the trainer's first choice for most of the horses in his barn. The lesson is that as important as a driver is, handicapping the horse's past performance is the priority. Another problem is that in cases where the driver can move the horse up a couple of lengths, the public bets entirely too much money on the driver change, and the bet becomes an underlay.

Thinking a horse will always improve with a better trip

Sure, if a horse has a better trip it will be more competitive, but what are the horse's chances of a better trip? Many horses have a certain style of racing that is ingrained in them, and they will never change. A horse may seemingly be going three wide every time it races, and if it doesn't go three wide tonight, it will probably win. But the horse may not have any early speed. With a closing style, the horse will usually be parked out a half mile and often go three wide and will seldom have a better trip.

Believing there is only one way to make money

Too often a beginner will think that there is only one way to make money at the racetrack, but the truth is that there are many paths to profits. What works for one person may not work for another. It is true that fundamentally all handicappers must be able to overcome the track take, but it can be done in several ways. It is important to seek profits by working with your strengths and avoiding your weaknesses. Professional athletes understand this well. Basketball players who have great rebounding skills do not spend their time shooting three-point shots. Baseball players who hit for power do not waste their time with bunting skills. Much of this seems obvious, but a handicapper that cannot succeed with a certain type of race or betting method should not attempt it. Using myself as a good example, I have problems with several areas of harness racing. Certain race types I cannot beat, but I continued to bet these races for several years. My records clearly showed that I was losing, but my ego was too big to accept the fact that I could not win playing these races.

You don't have to bet every race. In fact, you don't have to bet any at all. Pick your spots. This is much easier to do when you have several racetracks to choose from. It is much like a hitter in baseball who looks for a particular pitch in his hitting zone. When he sees the pitch, he swings hard.

Knowing which races I cannot win was a big step for me as a harness handicapper, but there have been other weaknesses that I have had to overcome. I only point these out to help you understand that you too can improve your handicapping by recognizing your weaknesses. Avoiding the weakness in your game and playing to your strengths can turn you from a losing player to a winning one, or if you already are in the black, it will make your profits rise.

Not having enough time to handicap but still making bets

Years ago, if I did not have enough time to handicap all of the races or handicap them properly, I would still end up making bets that I shouldn't have made. Oddly enough, having learned this lesson from attending the local race track, I had to relearn it with satellite wagering. Back in the days when there was only the local track to bet on, I would be running behind schedule and would not spend enough time with the program. With satellite wagering, I would often push myself to handicap all of the cards available. In other words, if there were six tracks to bet on and I only had time to handicap four of them, I would push myself to handicap all six programs; this would reduce my profits considerably. In some cases, it would turn a wining night into a losing one. Now, of course, I only handicap what I have time for.

Relying too much on numbers and ratings to pick winners

Relying too much on numbers such as pace, speed and class ratings to pick winners is a big mistake. Figures overrun your handicapping and your thinking. Horses become numbers, and this does not reflect reality. In the beginning, when I was first learning to handicap, the greatest value using figures had for me was that they helped slow down my handicapping. Beginners rush through the process of handicapping and miss important information. This in turn leads to the thought that you had the winner, but you made a mistake in handicapping the race. If you only would stop making mistakes you could crush the races and make a fortune. This, of course, is simply not true. A good understanding of the race will lead to a good bet or simply passing the race. Making mistakes because you go too fast is a sign of a poor handicapper, not a good one that needs to slow down. Make sure you understand as much about the race as your ability will allow and learn as you go.

Not betting to my strengths

By keeping accurate records, it was clear that I made money on both win and place wagering, but I had a better return on investment with my win betting. Clearly, it made more sense to only bet to win. But when I bet only to win, my return fell off to zero, and in some circumstances, I was losing money. The reason was that betting to win was simply not compatible with my personality. The place bet was a backup for the win bet and provided me with enough psychological security that I could handicap effectively. Without this mental security, I made too many mistakes in handicapping a race program. Unfortunately, my ego would not allow me to accept this situation, and I continued to attempt to make a profit betting to win only. It was if I thought I wasn't a good handicapper unless I could show a profit betting to win only. Of course, with time and maturity, I realized this was silly. Why lose money betting to win, if I can make a lot of money betting to win and place? As I got older, it no longer bruised my ego to admit I couldn't bet to win only. The same held true for betting exactas. Although I have hit some monster exactas in the past, the losing streaks were much longer than in the straight pools, and my psychological temperament could not handle it. The lesson for me was to play to my strengths and avoid my weaknesses. This meant knowing what kind of player I am and playing within these boundaries.

Section 8

My method

My method is fundamentally the same as all successful harness handicappers. I eliminate certain horses as non-contenders then compare the contenders. Each person has their own list of which horses should be thrown out, and the contenders are then judged on speed, pace, condition or class. Each handicapper will emphasize one factor over another, depending upon their favored approach to handicapping. My preference is with class, but I do place a strong, but secondary, emphasis on pace.

The following is my method explained as well as possible. For beginners, it will be disappointing because it is not a mechanical system that anyone can adapt. But this is how handicapping works. It is no different from anything else in life. There is no formula, but only hard work to develop the skills needed to succeed.

Handicapping begins with the condition of the race. Certain races will stress certain handicapping factors over others.

Races I do not handicap

I do not bet trotting races

Trotting races are just too frustrating. They break their gait more than pacers do. It is hard enough to handicap a race without trying to figure if a horse is going to break and how that will affect the rest of the field during the race. At one time I limited my handicapping of trotting races to those for older trotters, but even then it was only for the top half of the class hierarchy at the racetrack. Although I did better with my wagers, it was simply not worth the trouble.

I do not bet two year olds

In my opinion, two year olds should be non-wagering events. These horses are still learning the basics of racing and are too erratic. Not only do they have problems with breaking their gait, but they can improve overnight and make the race look like it was fixed. Two year old races are bad for my wallet, and as pari-mutuel races, they are bad for the sport.

I do not bet races carded at distances other than one mile

Odd distance races I completely ignore. You see this type of race at Yonkers where they will card a 1 1/16 distance race. The pace is a little slower, and I refuse to handicap a race where I have to factor in the horse's ability to go today's distance the way I would with a thoroughbred race.

Races I seldom bet

Maiden or non-winners of one race

Because I am a class handicapper, it is difficult to establish a horse's current ranking in the hierarchy if it has never won a race. I will occasionally find a wager in a maiden race, but not often enough to make it worth my time handicapping. However, those carded with a claiming price are simply too cheap to handicap. Many of these horses will never win a race. At least, they will not win at the current track they are competing at. There may be another track that has a lower class of maiden claiming category.

3 year old stakes races

These are difficult for me to handicap because I am dependent on eliminating horses to provide an advantage over the game. However, with three year olds pacing for large purse money, every trainer has their horse in top condition. A couple of horses can be eliminated for class, but the rest are contenders. There are simply too many horses in contention for my method to show a profit. I usually don't find a wager here, and when I do, it is usually one or two horses that are a class above the rest and are in sharp, but the class advantage will be obvious, and the horses will go off at low odds.

Elimination races

These types of races often will have the top 3 to 5 horses advance to a final race. Although the purse of the race is healthy, the goal is to make it to the final and winning is secondary to qualifying for the final race.

Bottom level claiming races

With rare exception, I do not bet the bottom level claiming races for a particular track. The reason is that most of them have a string of races at this level, and they have all shown themselves to have failed at the level two or more times. These same horses can also show several good races at this level. In short, I can make an argument for listing two-thirds of the field as contenders, but I could, with the same race, argue that they should all be thrown out. Horses at the lowest end of the spectrum can be difficult to handicap, and I find it difficult to make a profit betting them.

The one exception to this is when there is one horse that has only a couple of races at this bottom rung claiming level, and they were good races. This type of horse will usually have a slight class edge. Of course, everyone can see this, and the odds are low. A good bet is often a horse that is dropping to this level for the first time, or at least dropping to this level from its last eight to 10 races. These horses often don't look great on paper and will have better odds than a horse that shows a good race at this level.

Guidelines for Elimination

When I eliminate a horse from contention, I am not throwing the horse out as one that will not win the race so much as I am discarding the horse as one that I will not bet on.

Although I have rules for eliminating horses as contenders, most of them center on my conclusion about their condition or insufficient class for today's race. However, there are certain basic eliminations I do make.

At least two weeks between races

In other words, a horse can skip a week of racing and unless I know that the horse was scratched sick, I will ignore the missing week. The programs are pretty good at noting a scratch due to being lame or sick. I won't consider a horse that has missed more than two weeks of racing. It cost money to stable and feed a horse. If the horse is healthy enough to compete, it will be racing.

Last race was a qualifier

This is for older horses that have won races in their past. Occasionally one of these horses will bite you, but for the most part they are not ready to win off a layoff. That is assuming that was the reason for the qualifier. If it was because of a breaking problem, then it is rare for this type of horse to win. Often a horse will have a qualifier and show fast final times in its past performance. The horse is usually all out and will not pace as well in tonight's race. The old rule of thumb is a horse that is sharp off of its qualifier will pace a full two seconds better than its qualifying race time. This is generally true, and these are the types of horses that can win, but they are usually younger horses in non-winners of one or two races. Unfortunately, they are usually bet down heavily. Older horses with these strong qualifiers can also be bet down, but because they are weaker propositions, they create overlays in the rest of the field.

Eliminate a breaking horse that did not have an excuse

Betting on horses that broke in their last race is a poor wager. Unless it was clearly due to interference, it is a sucker's game to project victory if the horse stays on stride. Even if the horse is pacing well, the trainer may instruct the driver to take it easy with the animal making sure that the horse does not break. This is often the priority over winning a race. Another exception I make, although not seen often, is when a horse breaks at the start but still paces a good race. The horse may have finished in the money or finished within two or three lengths. As long as this is the only break in the last eight to ten races, or in the last three months, I may consider the horse for further evaluation. What I don't want to bet on is a situation where the horse figures to have the best chance of winning if it stays on the gait.

Eliminate horses that are not in shape

I want to see that the horse is in shape to win tonight's race. The horse may have finished poorly in the race, but I want to see that the driver attempted to win the race with the horse. Perhaps the horse took the lead and set too fast of a pace, and then dropped back only to finish poorly. The horse may have been parked without any cover or was parked with cover, and then showed a good finish. Maybe the horse was on the rail for the entire race, but closed some in the stretch. Often a horse will look bad on paper showing nothing until the stretch only to finish 6th, or 7th or generally speaking, in the rear half of the field, but when looking at the lengths gained in the stretch and the finish, the horse was clearly in good shape.

Eliminate horses that do not fit for class

The class of the horse is intrinsic to the class of the race. A horse needs to be placed at a level it can be competitive.

Being competitive in a race is a part of determining the fitness factor, but the horse must be properly placed in a race so it has a decent chance to win. Simultaneously, I am looking for horses whose overall class is equal to or greater than today's class level. I am mostly interested in whether a horse fits in today's race and not so much if the horse fits with the other horses. In general, I am looking for horses that are in shape to pace a good race and placed at their proper level by the trainer.

Along with shape, class is my main elimination for harness racing. This is why I consider myself to be a class handicapper. A horse's current form is fundamental to any approach to handicapping a harness race, but it is through the window of class that I handicap a race.

I go back at least eight races, but I prefer 10 to 11 races to judge how well a horse fits tonight's race for class. Given tonight's class level, I then compare each horse's last eight races for how well they performed at tonight's level or lower. Any race paced against better competition is ignored. Unless a horse had an excuse for its poor or mediocre performance, I want to see a competitive result from its race. This means the horse finished first, second, third or within three lengths of the winner. It doesn't matter how hard or easy the race was. If a horse's finish position fits this criterion, then it had a competitive result in the race.

I will allow a horse to have one uncompetitive result, but if the horse has two or more uncompetitive races, it is eliminated from consideration for betting. If a horse had an excuse for the result of the race, I will ignore the race. There are many excuses for a poor performance in a race. The following is a list of common reasons: a bad post position, off-track, the first race back after a layoff, the last race before a layoff, a trainer change, interference and broken equipment.

This list is not exhaustive and other items can be added. The principle is that there was a reason the horse was not able to demonstrate a competitive result. I allow one race to be excused without explanation because not everything can be explained reading the past performances.

Using the technique I have outlined avoids the mistake of determining a horse's class outside of a time frame that no longer applies. There is nothing permanent about the class of a horse. What the horse has achieved long ago may no longer apply. Going back eight to ten races will allow an analysis that is long enough to determine current class, but not so far back as to no longer apply.

Compare pace ratings of the horses that are left

At this point it is entirely possible and happens more than once on any given program, that I have no contenders. The entire field has been eliminated. In this case, I obviously pass the race. If the number of contenders in a race is too great, I will also pass the race. I must be able to eliminate the track take and have a healthy percentage in my favor. This is not going to happen by comparing five or six contenders. I am looking to throw out more than half of the field to give me a chance at a profit. The one exception is if I have eliminated the favorite. A horse that is going off at 2-1 or lower odds represents enough money in the pool to give me a strong positive expectation in my handicapping.

With a manageable field of contenders, perhaps two to four or even five in a field of nine or ten, a comparison can then be made between them. At this point I will use pace ratings to help determine each horse's chances of winning. Ignoring how the race will be paced, because this is the final step in my handicapping, I am simply looking at how good a performance a horse looks to be able to produce given its current condition and class level. In short, what is each horse's potential tonight.

I attempt to put a numerical value on this performance. This rating is a combination of the half mile time and the final time with a track variant added to it. I keep things simple by using the well known rule of thumb of one fifth of a second per length, so a horse's half mile time is the half mile fraction listed in the past performances plus one point per length behind in the race. A half or three-quarters of a length is rounded up.

I start with a one minute being equal to zero and then computing the fraction from this point. By quick example, if the race was paced in 0:58 to the half and a horse was three lengths behind the leader, this would be equal to seven points. Two full seconds is 10 fifths minus three lengths behind at the half is seven points. The same is done with the final time for the horse. In most programs they will compute a horse's final time for you. With the final time I use 2:00 as zero and compute how many fifths of a second under this time a horse paced. Again, one-fifth of a second equals one point. Track variants are either added to this pace figure or subtracted depending upon if the track that day was fast or slow. It is important to use one and a half times the variant because the half mile fraction is being added to the final time. If the track variant is -6 for a certain day, then I take 1.5 times -6, which is -9, and subtract this from the basic pace rating. If the track variant is an odd number, I take half of the number and round down. For example, a -7 would be a total of -10. Faster or minus variants are subtracted and positive or slower track numbers are added to the pace rating.

I don't bother modifying these ratings in any way because it is important not to use them as a magical formula to pick winners. The idea is to get an idea as to what the odds of the contenders should be. High numbers can be downgraded if they were done easily while other ratings can be better than they look because a horse was parked out or paced on the lead for one or more quarters. Post position has an obvious effect on these pace ratings. A horse moving from the inside to the outside will most likely pace to a slower number tonight. Horses who struggled from the outside in their last race may pace much better tonight with a favorable post switch.

The last step - Determining how the race will unfold

Picture in your mind how the race will develop. If you have been watching races for a long time at a particular track, you will be able to do this. There are many possibilities as to what can happen in a race, and when I picture the race in my mind, I am not so much looking at a scenario to determine a winner, but to look at the possibilities of how the race will unfold and influence my contenders. If I have a contender who will be shifting out three or more post positions and this horse has a lot of early speed, there may be enough early speed inside of the horse to force a fast first quarter to get the lead. If the horse has never shown the ability to win from off the pace, the chances are he will be sent early. But a trainer may decide not to rough his horse up and instruct the driver to take back early and attempt the win from off the pace. This will probably result in an off-the-board finish.

Keep in mind that horses that have been eliminated as contenders need to be included in determining how the race will be paced. A horse may not be a contender for the win, but could heavily influence the race and help one contender more than another. At this point, I may pass a race. This is especially true if the top contender projects to have a difficult time getting a good position in the race or will suffer a lot of pressure if he goes to the lead. A top rated closer that looks to have a slow first half to in the race will also be in a tough position to win. This is also the time to include your knowledge of drivers. A horse may be in great shape to win and has been placed at its proper level, but the animal's chances of winning can be compromised with a mediocre or poor driver. Often the driver's skill may not fit the animal's style of pacing.

Section 9

Betting on a Horse

Although this is my last step in the handicapping process, it is one of the most important. It represents what true handicapping is all about: taking what you know and applying it to the race at hand. You look at each contender's potential performance and then look at several possibilities of how the race will be paced. Each horse will have a certain probability of winning. You then take these probabilities and covert them to odds, limiting the wagers to those horses that are overlaid on the tote board.

There are some successful handicappers that make odds for all of their contenders and bet the one that is an overlay. Sometimes more than one horse can be bet if there appears to be more than one horse that is overlaid in the betting. I have problems doing this. Although I have been able to show a small profit betting on more than one horse, it has never been significant. Percentage wise, when I am at my best betting two or three horses, my advantage over the game is in the low single digits.

When I decide on a bet, I will focus on the horse with the best chance of winning versus the odds that the horse is going off at. I mostly bet equal amounts to win and place as this fits my temperament. If I have done a good job of eliminating poor bets from the field, I can almost bet on anything that is left. Granted, I will make mistakes in eliminating horses as well as including horses as contenders when they are not, but when looking at the big picture, I will show an advantage over the game.

An important conclusion on handicapping methods

Some handicappers do not place much emphasis on class; instead, they see the game through the window of pace, speed or perhaps only the shape of the horse. Whatever looking glass you have, always remember that you must stress picking losers and not winners. By picking losers accurately enough, you turn a negative expectation game into a positive expectation game. You become like the casinos in Las Vegas. The advantage in the game belongs to them. All they need to do is make sure there is no cheating, so the game is fair. When this happens, the more money bet by the players, the more money they will make.

Section 10

Final Thoughts

Although I show an excellent 15 to 20 percent advantage over the game today, the road to this point in time was rockier than it needed to be. Looking back to those first 5 to 10 years with harness racing handicapping and having an opportunity to learn all over again, I would have focused on a narrow area of harness racing and became an expert on it. If I could not have shown a profit on a certain type of race, I would have moved on to another area of harness racing. If I could have shown a profit, I then would have built upon that success and expanded my area of expertise.

Always remember that it is a game and enjoy playing it

There were times I became obsessed with beating the game and lost sight of how much fun harness racing can be. Try and enjoy the races as much as possible, but even if you're out to have a good time, you need to keep your losses to a minimum. If you are looking for a great hobby that is a lot of fun, a skilled harness handicapper can have a hobby that pays for itself.

ABOUT THE AUTHOR

Doug Masters has been handicapping horse races for more than three decades. Although most of this time was spent at racetracks, today Doug Masters makes his home in Las Vegas spending his time handicapping and betting on tracks throughout the country.

Douglas Masters

Other publications from Teela Books

Sports and Horse Racing Betting Systems That Work! by Ken Osterman

The book contains some of the best sports betting systems from Ken Osterman. These are systems that he has used himself successfully at both racetracks and sports books. The rules for each system are clearly explained and the systems are explained clearly so it is understood why they work. Tips for improving these systems are also provided.

There are 10 systems in this book that cover horse racing, football and baseball. Here is a list of the systems with the sport that is covered and the title of the system.

Horse racing

Quarter Horse - The Hidden Speed Horse Angle

Thoroughbred - Best Jockey – Long shot Method

Thoroughbred - Bet the Fastest Horse

Thoroughbred - Show a profit down under

Harness - The qualifier advantage

Harness - Morning Line Overlay

Sports Betting

NFL Football - The Injured Star

NFL Football - The Hat Trick

Baseball - The AAA Surprise

Baseball - The Underdog Advantage

This book is currently available:

In Kindle format on Amazon:

http://www.amazon.com/dp/B00JTMWDNM

It is also available on iBooks, Barnes & Noble, Kobo, Inktera, Scribd, 24Symbols, and Tolino.

It is also available in Paperback on Amazon

http://www.amazon.com/dp1507800142

The Path to Harness Racing Handicapping Profits by Douglas Masters

The Secrets of Harness Race Profits Revealed!

This book represents three decades of handicapping and betting harness races and is a summary of observations that are important to being a winning player. This book summarizes the conclusions on what made the author a winning player. There is no magic formula to become a winning player and the author is the first to say that there is more than one road to profits. This book is the road taken by Doug Masters to becoming a winning player. Becoming a winning player is part art and part skill, so it is impossible to summarize it as a mechanical method; however, Doug attempts to outline his process in the second half of the book.

This book may be difficult for beginning harness handicappers to read because it does not explain any basic terminology. There are, however, glossaries of harness racing terms online as well in the racing programs of harness tracks.

There are no winning examples in this book.

This is a quote from the author in the introduction.

"You will find no past performances listed in this book; this is intentional. Anyone who has been around harness racing for even a few years has probably read various books and publications offering a handicapping system. All of them will have examples of how a handicapping system or angle picked a winner. Anyone can do this, especially when so many of these authors are working backwards from the winner. To me, it is simply a waste of time. And besides, only a mediocre or inexperienced handicapper is going to believe there is a single path to success in wagering. This book consists of my observations of the sport and how it relates to my own handicapping perspective. If you are looking for a system that represents some sort of absolute truth, you're looking in the wrong place."

Topics include: Handicapping Factors, Drivers, Horse Form, Speed, Pace, Class, Post position, Track, Statistics, Betting multiple racetracks.

This book is currently available:

In Kindle format on Amazon:

http://www.amazon.com/dp/B00I5B13MU

It is also available on iBooks, Barnes & Noble, Kobo, Inktera, Scribd, 24Symbols, and Tolino.

It is also available in Paperback on Amazon

http://www.amazon.com/dp/1508707553

Type 2 Diabetes: From diagnosis to a new way of life

by Matthew Lashley

From the author

This book tells the story of how my diabetic condition was discovered, my denial of the condition, then the work done to get my glucose level to levels that are close to normal. There is no magic solution to treating type 2 diabetes, but I hope the information that I gathered and applied to my own life may be helpful to everyone struggling with type 2 diabetes. There is no cure, and I will have this condition the rest of my life. However, type 2 diabetes can be treated and controlled with the proper approach and lifestyle changes. You can have a better quality of life with a diet that is compatible with this disease.

Topics include:

From denial to self-blame

How I found out what type 2 diabetes was

Acceptance and getting down to work

Medication

Type 2 diabetes is a serious illness

How many carbohydrates per day should the limit be?

My target glucose levels

Foods to eat and foods to avoid

The importance of fiber in the diet

Eating out at restaurants

Is the damage from type 2 diabetes reversible?

Can type 2 diabetes be prevented?

This book is currently available:

In Kindle format on Amazon:

http://www.amazon.com/dp/B00IRJ9L1K

It is also available on iBooks, Barnes & Noble, Kobo, Inktera, Scribd, 24Symbols, and Tolino.

It is also available in Paperback on Amazon

http://www.amazon.com/dp/1508826005

The Quick and Dirty NFL Football Handicapping Method By Ken Osterman

The purpose of this book is to explain a fundamental approach to making a profit betting on professional football games, especially for those with little time to handicap them.

This method will help you find an overlay in the point spread using the simplest and quickest method possible.

The Quick and Dirty NFL Football Handicapping Method teaches you how to create your own point spread for each game in the NFL.

Table of Contents

Douglas Masters

Mistakes to Avoid

Conclusion

This book is currently available:

In Kindle format on Amazon:

http://www.amazon.com/dp/B00NX9X81I

It is also available on iBooks, Barnes & Noble, Kobo, Inktera, Scribd, 24Symbols, and Tolino.

It is also available in Paperback on Amazon

http://www.amazon.com/dp/151202614X

Betting on Major League Baseball
The Underdog Method By Ken Osterman

The essence of any good baseball handicapping system is to find games to bet on that will result in long-term profits. In other words, finding overlays. The Underdog Method uses an approach to not only find these good bets, but does so by creating a money line that can be compared to the one offered by sports books.

Author and sports gambler, Ken Osterman, explains this system in an easy-to-understand way, and then uses an entire day of baseball games as examples. Each game is handicapped per the rules of the Underdog Method, and then a betting line is created. This line is compared to a specific sports book's money line. It is then decided, based upon specific rules, whether a good bet exists or not.

Although demonstrating the effectiveness of any betting system is limited in a book, the approach to Major League Baseball betting using the Underdog System is significantly different than the simple angles and methods seen elsewhere.

This book is currently available:

In Kindle format on Amazon:

http://www.amazon.com/dp/B01220NL8I

It is also available on iBooks, Barnes & Noble, Kobo, Inktera, Scribd, 24Symbols, and Tolino.

It is also available in Paperback on Amazon

http://www.amazon.com/dp/1515180646

Free Things To Do on the Las Vegas Strip A Self-Guided Tour By Matt Lashley

The Strip is world famous and not only for the casinos, but also for the many things to see and do. Of course, a lot of what you can do here costs money, but there are a number of things to do that are free.

This book is a self-guided tour, taking you step by step down the Strip to visit all of the notable free things to do. This excludes most of the photo opportunities, because the entire length of the strip is filled with places to take a photo of you, your friends and relatives. Only a few places of interest, directly in our travel path, are mentioned. Also, shopping sites have been excluded except for three unique stores of interest on the Strip.

The trip begins at the Welcome to Fabulous Las Vegas sign and ends in the downtown portion of Las Vegas Blvd. This is the old section of Las Vegas and is not considered a part of the Strip. I have included it to provide a complete Las Vegas experience.

This book is currently available:

In Kindle format on Amazon:

http://www.amazon.com/dp/B01EW6DWXY

It is also available on iBooks, Barnes & Noble, Kobo, Inktera, Scribd, 24Symbols, and Tolino.

It is also available in Paperback on Amazon

http://www.amazon.com/dp/1533524084

Stealth Betting Systems for Winning at Casinos by Luke Meadows

Stop Losing and Start Winning in Las Vegas casinos!

Author and casino gambler, Luke Meadows, explains his betting methods he uses in Las Vegas casinos in an easy-to-understand way. There are casino systems for the games of roulette, craps, blackjack, Let It Ride, and Keno. Mr. Meadows is convinced that your best chance of winning is small wins using smart gambling systems, and to do this without bringing attention to yourself – a stealth mode of casino gambling.

In all of this time Luke, like most of us, has experienced both winning and losing. Over time, his trips to Las Vegas have produced more profits than losses. The reason for this is his method of gambling at casinos. A method that he has honed and fine-tuned to the point where he has the best chance of winning, while at the same time, keeping his losses low.

This book is currently available:

Douglas Masters

In Kindle format on Amazon:

http://www.amazon.com/dp/B01KGSN63S

It is also available on iBooks, Barnes & Noble, Kobo, Inktera, Scribd, 24Symbols, and Tolino.

It is also available in Paperback on Amazon

http://www.amazon.com/dp/1537175939

For the latest information about our publications, along with articles by some of our authors, please

visit our website at

http://www.teela-books.com

Made in United States
North Haven, CT
01 October 2022

24853775R00055